IN GOD WE TRUST

IN GOD WE TRUST

5 ANCHOR POINTS *for* TURBULENT TIMES

STEVE D. WHITAKER, PhD
with MATTHEW D. MCGEE

Foreword by **Pat Williams**, *Senior Vice President and Co-Founder Orlando Magic*

HIGHERLIFE
PUBLISHING & MARKETING

Oviedo, Florida

In God We Trust—Five Anchor Points for Turbulent Times
Dr. Steve D. Whitaker with Matthew D. McGee

ISBN 13: 978-1-939183-95-8

Published by
HigherLife Publishing & Marketing, Inc.
PO Box 623307
Oviedo, Florida 32762
www.ahigherlife.com

TABLE OF CONTENTS

FOREWORD

I F YOU'RE READING this book, you're most likely a parent or a grandparent. Ruth and I are the parents of 19 children and the grandparents of 17. There's nothing more important in all the world to us than the children God has entrusted to us.

No one ever promised that parenting would be an easy journey. While there are wonderful moments of joy, there are also times of unbearable pain and heartache. We pray, and we worry. In our humanness, we are torn between preparing the path and preparing the person. We want life to be smooth and trouble-free for our offspring. However, you and I know from personal experience that the difficulties and moments of testing produce a depth of character needed to weather the toughest storms in life.

In our family, we always looked for allies to bolster our calling as parents. I'm not sure it "takes a village" to raise a child, but I have always been a fan of finding others who support and encourage me in this important work. Coaches, pastors, teachers, and community leaders all have much to offer. They can be role models you point your children toward. They can be mentors and wise counselors speaking words of truth into the life of a child in a way that is nearly impossible for a parent.

However, the research is compelling that no one has the power to impact the life of a child the way a parent does. Researcher George Barna, studied family and culture trends for decades. He says, "The facts have been indisputably clear: in assessing the impact of churches, schools, and parents, it is the latter who have the most dramatic personal influence on a child."[1] You and I are the most powerful influence, for better or worse, in the lives of our children.

The blessing of parenting is God-ordained.

The blessing of parenting is God-ordained. In Deuteronomy, we find what is called the Shema. It was the most important prayer prayed in a Jewish home. Jesus would most likely have recited these words while seated at His father's feet in the morning and in the evening. God insisted that parents impress this Truth on the hearts and minds of their children.

"Hear, O Israel: The Lord our God, the Lord is one! You shall love the Lord your God with all your heart and with all your soul and with all your might."[2] The Shema is the Great Commandment. The children of Israel uprooted their families and made plans to cross over and possess the Promised Land—a land flowing with milk and honey. Moses implored the people to treasure God's Word and teach the Great Commandment to their children and their children's children so they might prosper for generations to come.

This commandment is the central message the Creator gives to creation. It is the supreme principle that will allow the people to flourish. It is an all-encompassing declaration. It is the grand finale to a divine symphony.

Missing this message would mean the children of Israel won the battle but lost the war. If emancipation from the clutches of the Egyptian rulers was simply a means to an easier life, the Exodus was all for naught. The blessing of the Promised Land was not about temporal possessions. It was about an eternal promise.

Moses explains in no uncertain terms how they were to carry out the process of extending the blessing of God's faithfulness to successive generations. He taught them a simple lesson on how to pass the baton. It's a message as timely today as it was more than 5,000 years ago.

Deuteronomy 6:6–9 says, "And these words that I command you today shall be on your heart. You shall teach them diligently to your children, and shall talk of them when you sit in your house, and when you walk by the way, and when you lie down, and when you rise. You shall bind them as a sign on your hand, and they shall be as frontlets between your eyes. You shall write them on the doorposts of your house and on your gates."

In God We Trust: Five Anchor Points for Turbulent Times is designed to help you teach your children Truth in the midst of these tumultuous days. Most parents aren't prepared to do this on their own. They need resources, coaching, and guidance. I highly recommend this book to you. It is a terrific resource for every Christian parent and grandparent.

—Pat Williams
Senior Vice President and Co-Founder for Orlando Magic, Author, and Motivational Speaker

ACKNOWLEDGMENTS

*"Two are better than one, because they
have a good reward for their toil. For if
they fall, one will lift up his fellow. But
woe to him who is alone when he falls
and has not another to lift him up!"*

ECCLESIASTES 4:9–10

A NY UNDERTAKING THAT is worthwhile in life requires the work of more than one. So it is with the writing of a book. Without the friendship, commitment, and skill of others, this dream would not have become a reality.

Thank you to my wife, Tricia, the greatest encourager a husband could ever dream of having by his side.

Thank you to my daughter, Amanda, a talented researcher and writer who turned a few good ideas into some great chapters.

Thank you to Caleb and Stephen, my sons, who were patient when I wasn't available to watch sports with them or play golf on weekends because I was in my study, writing.

Thank you to Matt McGee, my skilled co-author, who managed the process flawlessly and helped me stay focused on the goal.

This was truly a team effort. I must say in particular that the efficient work and unselfish devotion of Matt and Amanda kept this project from languishing. They are gifted writers and brilliant thinkers. Thank you both for making this a joyful journey!

INTRODUCTION

By Steve D. Whitaker, PhD

*"If we fail to instruct our children in
justice, religion, and liberty, we will be
condemning them to a world without virtue,
a life in the twilight of a civilization where
the great truths have been forgotten."*

Ronald Reagan[3]

IT WAS A slow drift. I didn't wake up one day and recognize that traditional family values were under attack. The process was deceptively slow and nearly painless with regard to my day-to-day life.

However, when I step back and examine today's landscape of religion, politics, and culture with an objective eye across the past two decades, I am astonished. The pace of change and the gap that has widened between traditional family values and popular culture is remarkable.

TEMPESTUOUS WAVES

As recently as 2008, both Democratic candidates running for president of the United States held strong beliefs that marriage was meant to be between a man and a woman (even Barack Obama and Hillary Clinton as late as 2011 were against legalizing gay marriage).[4] Just five years later, Aaron and Melissa Klein refused to bake a cake for a gay wedding and were told they could face fines up to $200,000 for breaking the law.[5] In February 2015, a superior court judge ruled that a florist would face charges because she wouldn't provide flowers for a wedding that was contrary to her religious beliefs.[6] The pendulum had swung. The president, who once supported traditional marriage, now led the fight for gay marriage.

Another recent shift in American culture has been from capitalism to socialism. Capitalism places emphasis on private and corporate ownership of capital, whereas socialism, in its purest form, places emphasis on equal distribution of wealth. The government does this by controlling every aspect of the economy. This shift is gradually embedding itself into US politics.

In 2008, the co-chair of the Socialist Party USA was not enamored by the election of Barack Obama. He suggested that for months he had seen people with bumper stickers and placards calling Obama a socialist, and he wasn't buying it. He said the newly elected president was not a socialist, and probably was not even a liberal.[7]

In 2016, after decades of capitalism, socialism came into vogue. What was once a term of derision become a badge of honor in less than a decade. Right before our eyes, one recent presidential candidate—a self-avowed socialist—quickly rose to prominence in the polls, and throngs of millennials cheered him on.

In the Iowa caucuses, an overwhelming 84 percent of the 30-and-under crowd voted for socialist Bernie Sanders. Exit polls from New Hampshire found 85 percent support for the socialist among voters in the same age bracket.[8] What is going on? The next generation is no longer alarmed by the idea of socialism—they embrace it as the solution to America's woes.

FAITH UNDER FIRE

Author Joseph Bottum has lamented the dramatic decline of religious influence: "The death of the Protestant church is the central historical fact of our time: the event that distinguishes the past several decades from every other period in American history. Almost every one of our current political and cultural oddities, our contradictions and obscurities, derives from this fact: the Protestant church has lost the capacity to set, or even significantly influence, the national vocabulary or the national self-understanding."[9]

You need look no further than the local news to discover that the role of faith in a person's life has been not just marginalized but fanaticized.

In California, police went to the home of a seven-year-old boy to tell him he could no longer hand out handwritten Bible verses at lunch to his friends. According to Liberty Counsel attorney Richard Mast, who represented the family, the child's elementary school sent a police officer to his home to set the record straight. He told the parents in no uncertain terms that the boy's Christian activities must stop because someone might be offended by the Bible verses.[10]

In the days following the Orlando massacre at the gay nightclub Pulse, an attorney with the American Civil Liberties Union said, "Christian conservatives are responsible for the mass shooting at the gay bar (in Orlando) because your thoughts and prayers and Islamophobia created this anti-queer climate."[11]

THE SECOND GREAT CIVIL WAR

Why should the cultural decay and the decline of religious influence in society cause us concern?

The answer is simple. We must be concerned and become engaged because we are losing the battle for the hearts and minds of our children. Their thoughts, perceptions, and values are increasingly being shaped by the primary influences in their lives. Television, the Internet, and social media are molding the worldview of America's children in ways we never expected.

We are losing the battle for our children.

Parents may soon have less influence over what their children believe today than at any other time in history.

A recent study by Common Sense Media found that "[o]n any given day, American teenagers (13- to

18-year-olds) average about nine hours (8:56) of entertainment media use, excluding time spent at school or for homework. Tweens (8- to 12-year-olds) use an average of about six hours' (5:55) worth of entertainment media daily."[12]

James Dobson, founder of Focus on the Family, calls the battle within our culture the second great civil war and says children are the prize to the winner. "Those who control what young people are taught and what they experience—what they see, hear, think, and believe—will determine the future course for the nation. Given that influence, the predominant value system of an entire culture can be overhauled in one generation…by those with unlimited access to children."[13]

Sociologist Neil Postman observed, "In the age of advanced technology, spiritual devastation is more likely to come from an enemy with a smiling face than from one whose countenance exudes suspicion and hate. 'Big Brother' does not watch us, by his choice. We watch him, by ours. There is no need for wardens or gates or Ministries of Truth. When a population becomes distracted by trivia, when cultural life is redefined as a perpetual round of entertainments, when serious public conversation becomes a form of baby-talk, when, in short, a people become an audience and their public business a vaudeville act, then a nation finds itself at risk; a culture-death is a clear possibility."[14]

There is no shortage of apt descriptors for the problem—a nation at risk, a culture war, a looming storm, or the great divide. For the purposes of painting a picture for you, we have chosen to describe the problem as an approaching storm. Those of us from Florida understand the language of hurricane preparedness and storm warnings well.

Let us describe our prayer and goals for this book in the following ways.

1. *We want to challenge Christ-followers to gain a fresh awareness of an important problem.* If you feel fairly comfortable with the condition of our culture, we hope this book will test your presumptions. If you find yourself anxious about the shape of our society, we want to encourage you and provide a game plan for taking action on behalf of the generation that follows.

2. *We want to point you to a firm foundation.* The first and most important component of the foundation is understanding God's role in the affairs of men. The second component is an understanding of human history and the role of the Gospel.

3. *We want to help you form a grace-filled response to the overwhelming needs in our country.* Believers are called to be in, but not of, this world. We have an obligation to engage the culture. Conservative political theorist Russell Kirk said, "Without Christian culture and Christian hope, the modern world would come to resemble a half-derelict funfair, gone nasty and poverty-racked, one enormous Atlantic City."[15]

As you read, you will encounter five key anchor points that will help your family survive turbulent times. If we continue to ignore the problem or underestimate its potency, we do so to our own peril.

Thank you for taking time to read this book and consider its claims. We have tried to make it very practical for you to use. At the end of each chapter, you will find a brief summary containing the key scripture and main idea of the chapter. Also, the "Family Minute" section contains a brief discussion guide for you to use with your family to help create teachable moments. At the end of the book, you will find a list of helpful Scripture references, as well as a "Seven-Day Guided Prayer Journey" designed to assist you in praying through the ideas we have covered in this book.

We believe these five anchor points will equip you to face the fiercest storms and come out on the other side with a sense of unparalleled confidence and determination.

STEVE D. WHITAKER, PhD

CHAPTER 1

HURRICANE WARNINGS: KNOW THE PATH OF THE STORM

By Steve D. Whitaker, PhD

"No fire alarm rang with a clear signal of danger. No modern-day Paul Revere rode through the public square to awaken us from our slumber. Indeed, many of our citizen soldiers still don't know that everything they hold dear is under attack."

Gary L. Bauer[16]

THE LIGHT IN the kitchen was on. The coffee pot was brewing. The radio volume was turned down low so as not to awaken the family. For the previous several days, my parents had talked in hushed tones about something in the news, but as a middle-school boy I was neither concerned nor interested.

But something was strikingly different about this morning. As my dad sat quietly in the kitchen, he studied the coordinates of the storm. This was in the days before we had a 24-hour weather channel. He seemed to be creating a checklist. As I walked into the kitchen, he barely looked up from his work.

The voices from the radio news broadcast and the papers on the table quickly told me he was working on a hurricane map. It was in the late summer of 1979 in South Florida, and as I was about to learn, Hurricane David was racing toward my hometown, leaving unparalleled devastation in its path.

"It's a powerful storm, son," my dad said. "Several days ago, the island of Dominica took a direct hit. There were winds as high as a hundred and fifty miles per hour. Reports say that nearly forty people died, and more than 50,000 were destroyed. But that's not all."

He continued, "A day or so later, the storm turned on the Dominican Republic as a Category Five hurricane. Wind speeds were measured at 175 miles per hour, and the waves were as high as twenty to thirty feet along the coast."

We lived in a small beach town in South Florida. His description of the storm struck fear into my young heart. My mind began to race as I considered his words. This was no ordinary weather event. As he took off his reading glasses and looked me in the eye, I knew instantly that he was worried for his family and the home he had built with his own hands.

My dad was a leader in our town, and I recognized that his concern extended beyond our family. He was thinking about what a storm like this might mean for our community. He was also deeply troubled by the loss of life throughout the Caribbean Islands. Since the early 1960s, he and several friends had invested time and resources to reach the people on these islands with the Gospel. Some of his closest friends were missionaries who now sat in the path of the hurricane.

On August 28, officials estimated that more than 1,500 people had lost their lives since the storm reached hurricane force. In Padres Las Casas, 400 people tied themselves together and attempted to make it to higher ground. In the midst of their climb, a dike broke, and they were washed away to a tragic death.

The next day, Hurricane David pounded the Bahama Islands and headed straight toward South Florida and our small community. The waves on the beaches were reaching dangerous levels. Homes were being evacuated. Rescue crews were shutting down streets. Our phone began ringing as friends and neighbors coordinated hurricane preparation efforts.

As the day wore on, I toggled between being gripped by fear and being caught up in the blur of activity. Would we survive? Would we lose our home and all of our earthly belongings? What about my friends? Would they be okay?

However, fear soon gave way to calm reassurance. As the hours passed, I watched my father methodically execute a plan to keep his wife and three sons safe during the next 48 hours of chaos. We boarded up the windows, filled milk jugs with drinking water, brought anything that might fly away indoors, and invited friends whose homes were in low-lying areas to ride out the storm in the safety of our home. God protected us through Dad's careful planning, understanding of the situation, and decisive action that exhibited a deep trust in God.

I grew up in a family grounded in traditional values. Church was an important part of my life. My community believed in the American dream.

We worked hard Monday through Friday. On Saturday we did our chores and enjoyed college football. Our front door was never locked. My dog wore a leash only when he was pulling me on my bike. My parents didn't track our every move on a "Find My Friends" app, and somehow we always made it home in time for dinner without the benefit of a reminder text message.

Political parties were more party than political. We disagreed on occasion, but the differences weren't such that the foundation of our culture seemed to quake.

The notion of civil discourse and adherence to traditional values seemed to remain stable through the turn of the century. As recently as the 2000 presidential election, both candidates struck a conciliatory chord on traditional values. It angered *The New York Times* so badly that one pundit wrote, "When the Kansas Board of Education removed evolution from the science curriculum testing to make way for creationism, neither Gore nor Bush could bring themselves to utter a word in defense of scientific truth."[17]

In that same election year, Al Gore said that when facing a difficult decision, he would often ask himself, "What would Jesus do?" After that, the acronym "WWJD" became iconic.[18] George Bush said in one of the presidential debates, "When you turn your heart and your life over to Christ, when you accept Christ as the Savior, it changes your heart. It changes your life. And that's what happened to me."[19]

All that was the calm before the storm. Since then, a storm of cataclysmic proportions has been brewing on the horizon. Wearing a WWJD bracelet seems an impossible notion for a presidential candidate today. If a political leader should dare pledge allegiance to the King of kings and Lord of lords, he or she would be scoffed at, labeled as dangerous, and deemed unfit for office.

The unrest and tumult within our culture have left a furrow on my brow like the one I saw on my dad at the breakfast table in August 1979. Like him, I have been studying the path of the storm and preparing a survival plan.

The approaching storm has two elements of concern: our churches and our communities. Both the community and the church are being battered by the winds of change. The forces of evil have aligned themselves and have taken aim at all we hold dear.

OUR CHURCHES ARE IN TROUBLE

Statistics show that the number of faithful church-goers is steadily declining. The only increase noted in the recent Pew Research Center study on religion was among the "nones"—a group that has made it their habit to reject denominational labels and church affiliation altogether.[20]

One-fifth of the US public—and a third of adults under 30—are religiously unaffiliated today. Those are the highest percentages ever recorded.

Scott Thumma, director of the Hartford Institute for Religion Research, says, "Everyone is trying to attract new people and hold on to them and make them disciples. But, today, people are seekers and shoppers looking for a temporary experience of worship, not a long-term commitment."[21]

Historically, church attendees shared a common set of beliefs and practices based on the Bible. The principles of Scripture guided the way we raised our families and related to our neighbors.

Most experts believe that since Johannes Gutenberg invented the printing press, five billion copies of the Bible have been produced. More than 90 percent of Americans are estimated to have a Bible in their homes.

In spite of this, the American Bible Society recently published a report suggesting that while we are buying copies of the bestseller at record rates, we're not necessarily buying into its message.

A majority of the Bible owners in the study said they are not interested in following its teaching. One-third of those between the ages of 18 and 48 said they never read the Bible. In an irrational turn of events, this same group (Bible owners) said America was in decline because of negative influences from secular media, corporate greed, and (wait for it…) lack of Bible reading.[22]

The decline of both biblical literacy and a Christian worldview have grave consequences for our nation. Nancy

Pearcey wrote the book *Total Truth* in which she dealt with this very issue. Her thesis is that we have lost our culture, and we are losing our children because young believers have not been taught how to develop a biblical worldview.[23] The Bible is prominently displayed on the coffee table but has very little impact on how we live our lives.

Friedrich Nietzsche famously said the church (those of us who call ourselves Christians) are to blame. "You have caged God, tamed him, domesticated him, and the priests have pliantly lent their aid. The roaring bull has become a listless ox. You have gelded God!"[24]

You and I have work to do.

You and I have work to do. We must become more active in our local churches, and we must respond with a renewed passion for the Bible as the only hope for a lost world. Nations have banned it, tyrants have burned it, and skeptics have scoffed at it. No other book has faced such opposition. Yet the Bible remains the standard for Truth, and His church will prevail. "The grass withers, the flower fades, but the word of our God will stand forever."[25]

COMMUNITIES AND CULTURE IN CRISIS

When the light of the Gospel is dimmed and moral relativism is lauded in the public square, we begin to see the unimaginable take place. The virtues that bound us together and the traditions that marked our civil society quickly evaporate.

Philosopher Will Herberg said, "We are surrounded on all sides by the wreckage of our great intellectual traditions. In this kind of spiritual chaos, neither freedom nor order is possible. Instead of freedom, we have the all-engulfing whirl of pleasure and power; instead of order, we have the jungle wilderness of normlessness and self-indulgence."[26]

The practical implications of the crisis are seen in every neighborhood across America. Businesses are no longer free to operate in a manner consistent with the conscience of the owner, and public schools have fallen victim to political correctness run amok.

The Orlando community was stunned when a volunteer chaplain for a local public high school football team was banned from continuing to serve dinner to the players and praying for them at the pregame meal.

According to reporter Todd Starnes, "The school district's crackdown on Christianity is the result of a lawsuit filed by the Freedom From Religion Foundation." He further added that an Orange County Public School (Orlando) memorandum stated, "Having a team chaplain is not permitted as it is an unconstitutional endorsement of religion in the same manner as a school employee participating in prayer with a student."[27]

Here's a brief primer on prayer in schools. Prayer was banned from public schools in 1962. The ban was reaffirmed and broadened to include graduation ceremonies in 1992. In 2000, the courts outlawed student-led prayer at public high school football games.

So what has happened in public high schools since the 1962 ruling of *Engel v. Vitale*? One author writes, "The elimination of the fear of God, symbolized by the Supreme Court's actions in the matter of school prayer, led to a dramatic increase in crime, venereal disease, premarital sex, illiteracy, suicide, drug use, public corruption, and other social ills."[28] The results speak for themselves.

Darryl Scott, father of a slain Columbine student, said this about prayer in schools while testifying before Congress: "Your laws ignore our deepest needs; your words are empty air. You've stripped away our heritage; you've outlawed simple prayer. Now gunshots fill our classrooms, and precious children die. You seek for answers everywhere and ask the question 'Why?' You regulate restrictive laws through legislative creed. And yet you fail to understand that God is what we need."[29]

As parents, one of our most important responsibilities is to interpret the world around us for our children. One of my goals is to help my children understand that they are growing up in a very different world than I did.

From the local high school to our nation's capital, traditional values are under attack. Rather than cursing the darkness, we need to light a candle and see these events as teachable moments for our children.

One teachable moment occurred when, after the Supreme Court legalized gay marriage, the White House was lit in rainbow colors. Planned Parenthood videos, which uncovered the sale of body parts of aborted babies, presented a teachable moment. The political rancor in Washington, DC, provides a wide range of teachable moments.

Teachable moments are not always pleasant and sterile. They are often difficult and troubling. However, these moments give us the opportunity to live out and reaffirm our faith in a changing culture. They give us the opportunity to teach our children important lessons of faith as it applies to daily life.

I don't know about you, but research like this leaves me discouraged until I consider the fact that God has promised to show Himself strong on behalf of His children, even in the most difficult times. The verse 2 Chronicles 7:14 promises us that "If my people who are called by my name humble themselves, and pray and seek my face and turn from their wicked ways, then I will hear from them and will forgive their sin and heal their land." God is faithful to carry out what He has promised if we are faithful to carry out our part.

THERE ARE MORE WITH US

At one of his lowest points in the War for Independence, General George Washington reflected honestly on his odds of winning. In doing so, his typically optimistic nature was tested beyond measure. He estimated that he had 8,880 men at hand, of whom fewer than 7,000 were able to fight. The enemy he faced was much larger.

He had just received word that the British had hired 17,000 Germans to fight against the Sons of Liberty and their followers. This brought the Red Coats' fighting force to nearly 30,000 by his best calculations.

Less than 48 hours later, more bad news was delivered. The British were moving against him by land and sea. At daybreak, enemy ships began appearing in the harbor. Some reports stated that on the morning of June 29 alone, 45 ships dropped anchor. By the end of the day, many accounts say that more than 100 enemy vessels crowded the bay at Staten Island.

On July 2, 1776, the Continental Congress pushed back and voted to terminate its relationship with Great Britain. It was a foolish move by any worldly measure. Many claimed it would be the kiss of death for the American cause.

David McCullough recounts this story in greater detail in his book *1776*: "At a stroke the Continental Congress had made the Glorious Cause of America more glorious still, for all the world to know, and also to give every citizen-soldier at this critical juncture something still larger and more compelling for which to fight. Washington saw it as a fresh incentive, and to his mind, it had come at not a moment too soon."[30]

We celebrate the brilliant determination of all those who fought to win our freedom as a nation. We also take hope and gain courage from their example in the midst of our present-day struggles.

Like Washington, we may feel overwhelmed. However, we find hope in 2 Corinthians 4:8, which says, "We are afflicted in every way, but not crushed; perplexed, but not driven to despair."

In the book of 2 Kings, we find the prophet Elisha surrounded by an enemy army sent for his capture. He is calm, but his servant is overcome with fear. I relate more to the servant.

"Early in the morning a servant of the Holy Man got up and went out. Surprise! Horses and chariots surrounding the city! The young man exclaimed, 'Oh, master! What shall we do?' He said, 'Don't worry about it—there are more on our side than on their side.' Then Elisha prayed, 'O God, open his eyes and let him see.' The eyes of

We are on the winning side.

the young man were opened and he saw. A wonder! The whole mountainside full of horses and chariots of fire surrounding Elisha!"[31]

We may be surrounded on every side. The political world may look worrisome. The pollsters may predict woeful outcomes. Our culture may seem headed for destruction. But we can say with confidence to our children, "There are more with us than are with them. We are on the winning side. We've read the last chapter of the book, and we know Who is victorious!"

CHAPTER SUMMARY

Our own personal experiences and the illustrations in this chapter leave us with a common understanding—we are facing some uncharted waters. The dangerous winds include moral relativism, political turmoil, and an all-out assault on religious liberty that can lead many of us to worry and become anxious. Lessons from this chapter call us to take the following actions:

- Plan carefully for the coming storm so that you and your family are prepared.

- Study the details of the storm thoroughly so that you're not surprised by its severity.

- Deepen your commitment to the local church, and invite others to join you.

- Develop a plan to study and apply the Bible and its teachings. It is okay to start small, but be sure to start.

- Understand that in times of turmoil, our neighbors are watching to see how Christ-followers respond.

- Find peace in the assurance that God is on our side. He is in control.

Key verse: "He said, 'Do not be afraid, for those who are with us are more than those who are with them'" (2 Kings 6:16).

FAMILY MINUTE

When Jesus was on earth, His message was met with resistance and persecution. He was mocked, scorned, and crucified. However, His message remained the same: love those who hate you, and do good to those who persecute you. If He walked among us today, He would still be serving, giving hope, and pointing people to the hope of eternal life. "For God so loved the world, that he gave his only Son, that whoever believes in him should not perish but have eternal life."[32] Although the world around us is changing, the message of the Gospel remains the same.

Read the story in 2 Kings 6:1–17 with your family. Ask the following questions:

1. Whom do you identify with more, the prophet Elisha or his servant? Why?

2. In what ways do you think Christians today might feel outnumbered like the servant?

3. How can we more effectively encourage one another to remember that there are more with us than are with them?

CHAPTER 2

ESSENTIAL PREPARATION: ANCHOR DEEP, AHEAD OF THE STORM

By Matthew D. McGee

*"Some trust in chariots and some in horses, but
we trust in the name of the Lord our God."*

PSALM 20:7

As a young Jewish girl, Anna always looked
forward to her wedding. Like most young girls,
she dreamt about what it would look like, from what
colors she would use in the ceremony to what type of

food would be served at the reception. Whenever she had a free moment, her mind would drift, and she would be transported to that occasion standing beside her groom. It could not arrive soon enough for her.

Finally, she met the man of her dreams, and her wedding day actually arrived. She had never been more excited. The man she married exceeded her wildest dreams. He was kind, hardworking, and tenderhearted. He had grown up just down the street from her. They had passed each other along the dusty streets of their town for years.

Only in God's beautifully designed plan could this have happened. Anna was overwhelmed by the generosity of God's gracious gifts.

The ceremony took place without a hitch. It went exactly as planned (with the exception of the donkey braying as they said their vows). Anna was incredibly thankful for the amazing blessings she was experiencing— an incredible husband, a home to share, and dreams of children who would one day join them.

Then one day unexpectedly, tragedy struck. Anna never saw this coming, and it certainly had not been part of her dreams as a young woman. Inexplicably, her husband passed away. What now?

She couldn't begin to imagine how her life could go on without her husband. How could she live as a widow, particularly in a culture where widows struggled to find work, make a living, or own property? Women without husbands were destined for lives of poverty and difficulty.

After all those years of waiting, she was forced to start over. It felt as if the rug of life had been pulled out from under her. Where would she turn? Could she go on? What hope was left? Anna's greatest trial would force her to find a source of hope.

THE SOURCE OF HOPE

If you ask many today, they will identify with Anna's search for hope. They simply don't have much of it when it comes to our culture, our country, or future generations. Our country, in which traditional values were once upheld and hard work was rewarded, is no longer recognizable to them.

Our financial systems have been devastated by corruption, and many of our politicians serve no one but themselves. Much of what used to provide a sense of security is a distant memory. America, at first glance, looks very different than it did even a few years ago. The question arises, "During these turbulent, storm-tossed times, how do we go forward? How do we make a life when all around us there is little to hope in, little that we can rely on?"

The famed Russian novelist Fyodor Dostoyevsky once said, "To live without hope is to cease to live."[33] This statement is more than just an inspirational quote on a coffee cup encouraging a person to keep his chin up. It encapsulates a basic human need.

Dostoyevsky understood the great evils of humanity and wrote extensively about them. He faced some of the most oppressive and corrupt government regimes of the modern era. He understood what it was like to be under a system that did not value what he valued. He understood how it hurt to see personal freedoms erode like sand castles facing stormy waves.

He also understood the reality that genuine hope is a must for life, even in the direst of conditions. It is a necessary anchor to which men and women secure their lives. Without it, we are unable to survive. Yet having a source of hope is just the beginning. It is not just having hope that matters; it is having hope in something that does not fail.

According to the *British Journal of Psychiatry*, between 2008 and 2010 there was a significant spike in suicides across America, Canada, and Europe.[34] This rise in suicides during this specific time period caused researchers to explore the potential cause.

They looked for something happening across these countries to explain why more individuals were giving up on life. The article goes on to explain that "There [had] been a substantial rise in suicides during the [economic] recession, considerably more than we would have expected based on previous trends."

The research revealed that for many, their entire source of hope was based on their financial position. When that hope crumbled, many found that their sole anchor had given way. They were left adrift with nothing to rely on or place their hope in.

Dostoyevsky understood that we must have hope in something to survive. The failing economy demonstrated that choosing the right object of our hope is just as important.

CHOOSE WISELY

There is an old story that tells of an inexperienced boat owner who, upon hearing of a coming storm, began to fasten his craft to the dock. He spent hours making sure the ropes were strong and each knot was secure. When

We must anchor deep.

the job was almost complete, a seasoned sailor walked by and informed him that, despite his best effort, the vessel was doomed for destruction. The magnitude of the coming storm meant that not even the dock was safe from destruction. The only hope for the man's vessel was to go out to sea and anchor deep.

Like the boat owner, we look frantically for a way to anchor the ship of our lives. We want to anchor our families to weather the impending storm, so we must anchor deep.

Our culture promises us many "docks," or avenues, for safety and security, from a multitude of sources. Entertainment and other media exist thanks to paid advertising. Take a moment and think about the nature of what commercials on television are really selling.

A recent television commercial by Audi addresses a theme many can relate to: the wish to live an exciting and unpredictable life. In this commercial, workers are stuck in a mundane rut, unable to escape.

The viewer senses the pain, agony, and lifelessness of these employees who yearn for more. It is not until the Audi SUV screeches onto the screen that the main character finds the power to break free, escape the monotony, and live the exciting life he always wanted.[35]

This car commercial never promotes any features of the car itself. It never highlights any particular safety feature. The only thing the commercial tries to sell is freedom from the tyranny of living according to the expectations of others. In essence, it is trying to sell a meaningful life.

Audi's goal is that you would place your hope in this car. They want you to "drop an anchor with them." Maybe if you drove this particular type of luxury car, then you would find the essence of life and be rescued from its banality.

Everyone says it's fun to drive a fancy new car, but relying on a vehicle as the source of joy in life will leave you desperate for something more. The manufacturer hopes to release another new car in about five years. Fifty years from now, all cars end up in the same place: the junkyard. There simply is nothing built by man that will live up to the expectation offered by this commercial.

Like this Audi commercial, advertisers know and strategically try to capitalize on the search for hope that consumes the human heart.

The children of Israel ran into this same dilemma throughout the Bible. God's people were constantly faced with a similar decision, a similar search. Sometimes they chose God and found a source of hope that would not disappoint. Sadly, many times they chose anchor points that failed when the storm came.

God described their poor choices like this: "For my people have committed two evils: they have forsaken me, the fountain of living waters, and hewed out cisterns for themselves, broken cisterns that can hold no water."[36] He reminded them sternly that He is the only true source of living water, of living hope. Anchoring in anything else is like trying to hold water in a cracked jar that holds no water.

WHEN DREAMS DON'T COME TRUE

This became very real to me in my freshman year of college. I had been a member of the Army ROTC and absolutely loved it. I dreamed of being commissioned as an officer and leading a group of soldiers. During our physical training, I excelled. I relished every moment of training. When the time came to sign the contract to commit, my medical clearance was rejected because of a childhood illness. I was "done in" and frustrated with God. I expressed my anger to Him quite boldly. In that moment, I had forgotten the source of my hope. It wasn't until five years later, as I was gratefully serving a church in Malaysia, that I fully understood why God allowed that difficult circumstance to come into my life.

WHEN LIFE FALLS APART

If hope is indispensable, the object of hope is just as crucial. Life's ultimate questions become "Where does one go to find a true source of hope? Is there a proven source of hope that is able to sustain even in the midst of the utmost difficulty?"

When I was growing up in church, we sang a classic hymn of the Christian faith. One beautifully written line describes what a relationship with God offers: "When all around my soul gives way, He then is all my hope and stay."[37]

This song eloquently says when everything else in life fails, and nothing in society gives us any sense of promise, God is our sufficient and satisfying source of hope. He will provide a stable foundation we can build our lives on.

Although many claim to be a source of hope for troubled times, there is only one Who has a proven track record and Who has demonstrated powerfully His ability to be the source of authentic, true hope. In the book of 1 Peter, chapter 1, verses 3 and 4, we are provided with the ultimate reason for this hope: "Blessed be the God and Father of our Lord Jesus Christ! According to His great mercy, He has caused us to be born again to a living hope through the resurrection of Jesus Christ from the dead, to an inheritance that is imperishable, undefiled, and unfading, kept in heaven for you."[38]"

These verses state that the reason our hope in Jesus is sure is because Jesus defeated death through His resurrection. Many religions present themselves as adequate sources of hope. However, there is only one Who has proven His worth in the face of life's greatest trial—death. Death is the ultimate hope destroyer. Death is final.

This verse continues to explain the benefits of this hope. Jesus not only conquered death by coming back to life, but He has prepared for us an "inheritance" in eternity. Our hope in Jesus is ultimately the promise of eternal life. Our inheritance is the promise that no matter what circumstances come our way in this life, Jesus gives eternal life to those who follow Him. This eternal life is secure. It can never perish, spoil, or fade.

We can trust God and rely on Him. He is a secure anchor point because He has proven Himself, and His character validates that He is who He says He is.

This leaves us with a choice. What will we do with this promise? We can ignore it, simply study it, or embrace it. If we anchor our lives to it, we are assured of security in not only this world, but the world to come.

What will we do with this promise?

HORSES AND CHARIOTS?

God designed the human heart to find hope in something. We are unable to go through life and hope in nothing. Some will argue that they do not need anything external; they rely on themselves. They have chosen self-reliance as their hope.

Many Americans have achieved great success and wealth as a result of hard work. However, this can all be undone in a moment. A diagnosis of cancer, Parkinson's, or Alzheimer's will reduce all of this worldly success to nothing. The real question is not *whether* we will find our hope in something, but *what* do we pursue to satisfy our hope?

As we navigate these turbulent times, we must constantly evaluate where we are placing our hope. Politicians, advertisers, self-help books, and religious leaders clamor for our allegiance, promising they will be the solution to our concerns.

Our concerns go much deeper than outward circumstances. We need a source of hope that is proven, true, and unchanging. There is only one source: the eternal God and a relationship with His Son, Jesus Christ.

"Some trust in chariots, and some in horses; but we will trust in the name of the Lord our God."[39]

Even with our hope placed in something substantial, we face challenges daily. There is still much that causes us to second-guess. It is in these moments that we must remember God's promises.

We must look to the Lord and remember that He is a promise-keeping God. We must remember that He has not failed yet. When all seemed hopeless and all was lost, Jesus rose from the grave.

I am reminded of the prayer in Romans 15:13: "May the God of hope fill you with all joy and peace in believing, so that by the power of the Holy Spirit you may abound in hope." I find great comfort in the knowledge that even when it seems futile to continue hoping, God is able to give us joy and peace. By the power of the Holy Spirit, we can persevere.

THE REST OF ANNA'S STORY

Anna was despondent over the loss of her spouse. Yet she did not lose hope that God was in control and had a plan for her life. The story of Anna is found in the book of Luke in the Bible. Although we don't have many details about the early part of her life, we know Anna had been a widow for almost eighty years. When we meet her, she had spent her life seeking God, making Him her anchor and her hope.

Proclaiming the Good News to all who sought a deliverer, Anna was there when baby Jesus was taken to the temple. Anna got an inside look at what God was doing. This privilege was afforded her because she kept her hope in her Deliverer and trusted that He would come through on His promises.[40]

Anna placed her hope in the promise of God, and He came through for her. Her life of devotion to God was not in vain. Many Bible stories like this give us confidence that God is a wellspring of hope and a fountain of living water. He will not fail us. He will not abandon us.

CHAPTER SUMMARY

The world has many ideas about what can give us hope and what should be our firm foundation in times of crisis. Some suggest that power will offer salvation. Others suggest that wealth and possessions can fortify us against oppressive forces. However, believers understand that only in Christ can we find true hope and security to sustain us through the most troubling times. He is the source of true life.

Lessons from this chapter call us to take the following actions:

- Use discernment in a world that offers empty promises dressed up as the answers to our problems.
- Understand the importance of placing our hope and confidence in our Heavenly Father.
- Read the Bible and identify examples of God's faithfulness.
- Persist, even when our trust is tested by a world that is no friend of grace.

Key verse: "Some trust in chariots and some trust in horses, but we trust in the name of the Lord our God" (Ps. 20:7).

FAMILY MINUTE

Jesus found His own trust tested. After 40 days of fasting and prayer, Satan tempted Him. When we face difficulty in our lives, we will be tempted and tested. We can learn much from the story of Jesus's encounter in Matthew 4:1–11. Read this passage with your family and ask the following questions:

1. What three temptations did Satan put before Jesus?

2. What is the weapon that Jesus used three times to resist temptation?

3. Pick one verse from the list of Scriptures at the back of this book and memorize it as a family.

CHAPTER 3

WHEN THE WAVES START CRASHING: PUT TRUST TO THE TEST

By Matthew D. McGee

"Know therefore today, and lay it to your heart, that the Lord is God in heaven above and on the earth beneath; there is no other."

Deuteronomy 4:39

Joseph had always been a promising child. From the time he could talk, he never met a stranger. He was charismatic, funny, caring, and compassionate. He was well liked by just about everyone. As if all of that were not enough, he was also a great athlete. From an early age, he could easily outrun most of the boys in his town.

Although Joseph was a dreamer, he didn't have ordinary dreams. Joseph dreamed big dreams. He had a sense that one day he would accomplish something significant with his life.

His nighttime dreaming corresponded to his suspicion. While he slept, he often found himself in situations that required saving the day, rescuing the hurting, and rising to greatness.

Joseph didn't quite understand that he didn't need to tell others about his frequent dreams of grandeur on a regular, repeating basis. It was this particular quality that caused annoyance among the rest of his family. What started out as an irritating trait of a little brother grew into something more.

MORE THAN A DREAMER

One person who looked past all of Joseph's faults was his father. He had a hunch that this child would be different. He could tell by the way his son walked and by the way he carried himself that God had something special in mind for Joseph.

Somewhat unwittingly, Joseph's father began to show favoritism toward Joseph. While he felt he was nurturing Joseph's God-given talent, the rest of the family did not see it that way. A little extra portion of dinner or an extra gift at the holidays eventually gave way to more obvious favoritism. Specially made clothes were given to Joseph, while the rest of his brothers had to fend for themselves or be content with hand-me-downs.

As you can probably imagine, this favoritism heightened problems in the household. Simple dislike for Joseph grew into outright hatred, which would ultimately lead to violence.

Joseph's family were shepherds. One day while the brothers were tending the sheep, Joseph's father sent him on a special assignment to check on his brothers. When they saw Joseph coming from a distance dressed in the fancy clothes his father gave him, they were reminded of their hatred toward him. They decided to take action.

Their first thought was to kill him and tell their father that a wild animal devoured him. Thankfully, cooler heads prevailed. They decided to "only" sell him to slave traders. Joseph's story took a few other dramatic turns as he was sold to one of the ruling-class members in Egypt.

The lowest point in Joseph's story found him in jail, falsely accused with no hope of a future.

Joseph met two others in jail, fellow prisoners who needed his help. These two prison mates had vivid dreams that Joseph interpreted for them. Because God had given him the ability to interpret dreams, Joseph's interpretations turned out to be completely accurate.

Eventually the Egyptian pharaoh heard of Joseph's gift and called his services into action. The ruler of Egypt had two very graphic dreams that haunted him. No one in his household could do anything to alleviate his anxiety. However, with God's help, Joseph was able to interpret the dreams, revealing that the entire nation of Egypt and the surrounding areas would soon enter a time of severe famine. Seeing that God was with Joseph, Pharaoh asked Joseph to help Egypt through this national danger as a community crisis manager. Joseph was promoted to second-in-command of the entire nation.

MEANT FOR EVIL

Because the famine spread throughout the entire region, Joseph's brothers went to Egypt seeking food. Ironically,

Joseph was in charge of selling all the food and was now in a position of authority and power over his brothers.

When his brothers arrived, they did not recognize Joseph, but he immediately recognized them. After several days' interaction, he eventually revealed his true identity. His brothers were dumbfounded and fearful of the retribution that Joseph could take out on them.

With loss, disappointment, and wasted years behind him, Joseph now had the authority to exact any type of revenge he chose. The brothers must have wondered if they would be killed or sent to prison.

Joseph's response becomes very instructive for us as we navigate our own personal and cultural storms.

In one of the most poignant verses in all of the Bible, Joseph illus-

We can respond with grace and love.

trates how his confidence in God's sovereignty enabled him to respond with grace and kindness. Joseph experienced the worst of circumstances, but his confidence in God's control allowed him to say to his brothers, "Do not fear, for am I in the place of God? As for you, you meant evil against me, but God meant it for good, to bring it about that many people should be kept alive, as they are today."[42] Joseph assured his brothers that in addition to his forgiveness, he would provide for them and their families during the famine.

From the life of Joseph, we see that God's sovereign orchestration of all circumstances should provide us with confidence. When we encounter those who disagree with us, we can respond with grace and love. No matter how dire the circumstances may appear, He is worthy of our trust, and we need not despair.

GOD IS GOOD, ALL THE TIME

Imagine being like Joseph, a young man full of hope and promise. Your dreams are dashed because you are thrown into prison without cause. God is not silent in the background; rather, He is working for good, even in our darkest times.

Joseph had no indication that God was present with him. He had no way of knowing that he would not only be released from prison but would ascend to the second-highest position of leadership in Egypt. During the lowest chapter of Joseph's life, he depended on his belief that God loved him and had not abandoned him.

As we survey today's political and moral landscape, it may seem there is little hope. However, the knowledge that God is in control and loves us will provide the greatest assurance on the most difficult days. Even if we see no way out, God is still working for our good and for the good of others.

TRUSTING GOD, NO MATTER WHAT

As a senior in high school, the last university I wanted to attend was the one in my hometown. I had dreams of driving several hours away to experience the thrill of college football and living in another state. The anticipated scholarship money did not come through, and I was dejected. Yet looking back, I can see clearly the story God was writing. I can see the good He had planned for me by having me stay in my hometown. I established a lifelong friendship as a result of attending the local university. I was able to intern at our church, which led me to go to graduate school for theological training. Best of all, I became better friends with the girl who would one day become my wife. All of this happened because God knew better than I did. My job was to trust Him.

TRUST HIS CHARACTER

Trusting God is not always easy, especially when the circumstances we are going through seem to indicate otherwise. But during these times, we must rely on God's promises instead of our circumstances as the interpreting guide.

When the stock market is going up and down more than a roller coaster at Six Flags, God is not surprised. When the web of politics seems to reward dishonesty, cronyism, and personal expediency, we trust that there is a more powerful Ruler in charge of the universe Whose character could never be questioned and Whose competency is sure.

Trusting in God's control over the affairs of mankind does not guarantee a pass on difficulty, nor does it guarantee that society will affirm and promote our deeply cherished values. Belief in God's sovereignty provides a foundation that does not shake. It assures us that not all is lost and that true good is coming. This is the battle, to trust the "long view" of God's plan.

A MUCH BIGGER PLAN

We may be tempted to view our current political or cultural difficulties as disconnected from the greater work and greater purpose of what God is doing. We see this pattern of action throughout the Bible and throughout history. With Joseph's story, God was up to something a lot bigger than one man's life.

Joseph was ultimately exalted to second-in-command over the land, but that wasn't all that God accomplished. God used Joseph to rescue an entire nation of people.

PERSECUTED, YET PROSPERING

From 1966 to 1976, Mao Zedong and his Communist Party carried out the Cultural Revolution across China.[3] In Mao's purge to rid China of all threats to Maoist ideology, Christians, among other groups, were severely persecuted. It was an open assault against any cultural or religious expression or freedom. It was absolutely harrowing for Christians. No longer could they openly worship. No longer could they follow Christ without fear of persecution from the Chinese authorities.

The church was forced to go underground and meet secretly. Any sign of Christianity on a building or in a public area was removed. At the beginning of this persecution, China had relatively few Christians compared to other countries. With such scant numbers, many doubted there would be any chance of survival for this small Christian population.

Something incredible happened.

Would Christianity go extinct in a country where it had just begun to flourish?

In the years since the Cultural Revolution, persecution of Christians has ebbed and flowed. Despite the tide of culture working against the church, something incredible happened—Christianity actually grew under this government threat. An article in a British newspaper provides an update on the status of Christianity in China today: "China's Protestant community, which had just one million members in 1949, has already surpassed that of countries more commonly associated with an evangelical boom. In 2010 there were more than 58 million Protestants in China compared to 40 million in Brazil and 36 million in South Africa, according to the Pew Research Center's Forum on Religion and Public Life."44

The article goes on to project that by 2025, the number of Chinese Christians will outnumber those in the United States.

How did the Chinese church grow under such intense persecution? When all the circumstances looked bleak, and the government was decidedly anti-Christian, removing any semblance of religious freedom, how did the Chinese church survive?

The Chinese Christians exercised absolute trust in His plan.

The only reasonable answer is that God was at work, and the Chinese Christians exercised absolute trust in His plan. Although they may not have been able to see it, God was working in the midst of extremely difficult circumstances. What the Chinese government determined would harm resulted in good. Amazingly enough, modern Chinese Christians believe that the presence of persecution serves to grow the church.

TRUST GOD'S SOVEREIGNTY

Imagine for a moment that the claims we have put forward were not true. What if God did not have a plan for good and He was not in control? What if He was unable to ensure that good would come out of even the most desperate circumstances? Fear and hopelessness would undoubtedly reign.

A lack of trust in God manifests itself most clearly in fear—fear of the future and fear of other people. This is a debilitating way to live. Fear affects the way we relate to our friends, family members, and communities. Where there is fear, there is often hate.

Joseph's trust in God's sovereignty allowed him to see people and circumstances differently. His belief that God was in control allowed him to show love and grace to his brothers. Instead of sending them to jail, he provided housing and food for them.

None of this would have been possible if Joseph felt his life had been ruined or his hardships futile. It was only when he was able to trust the hand of God that he was then able to serve and extend grace to others.

We all have areas in our lives where this is a struggle for us to believe and a challenge to live out. Whether it is in difficult circumstances financially, physically, or culturally, our trust is often tested.

These truths stir up important questions. Can we regard difficult people not as an enemy to be feared, but as people worthy of love and service? Who have we kept at a distance for fear that somehow he might take away or diminish the good things we cherish in our lives?

We see this kind of hatred most clearly in politics. We are so fearful of what the other side is doing or how they are influencing our country that we are unable to carry on a civil conversation with someone who holds an opposing viewpoint.

As individuals who believe God is in control, has a plan, and will never be conquered, we are free to love others no matter what—even when they vote differently, speak differently, or worship differently.

The only reason to fear or truly hate someone else is if you believe they have control of the outcome of your life. As we see clearly from the life of Joseph, God was in control, turning what others meant for evil into good.

CHAPTER SUMMARY

From the life of Joseph, we learn powerful lessons that allow us to rest in God's providence. When circumstances seem bleak and we don't see how we can survive, God may take what appears to be a temporal burden and turn it into an eternal blessing. Lessons from this chapter call us to do the following:

- Remember that God may use unbelievers to accomplish His purposes in our lives.
- Rest in the promises of God—they are new every morning and never fail (Lam. 3:22–23).
- Understand that we are part of a larger plan as God works to advance His kingdom on earth.
- Press on toward the prize even when faced with opposition and persecution.
- Trust God's sovereignty to work all things together for His good in our lives.

Key verse: "As for you, you meant evil against me, but God meant it for good, to bring it about that many people should be kept alive, as they are today" (Gen. 50:20).

FAMILY MINUTE

The story of Joseph is one of the most intriguing in all of the Bible. He began as his father's favorite son. His jealous brothers attempted to kill him. He was rescued, became a servant in a far country, and gained favor in the house of a powerful Egyptian official. He was then wrongly accused and banished to prison. However, because of his faithfulness, God rescued him and blessed his life in more ways than he could have ever imagined. His brothers showed up in Egypt to look for food before they starved. Joseph disguised his identity. He was torn between taking revenge and showing grace.

Read the summary above to your family. Then read the powerful conclusion to the story in Genesis 45. Ask the following questions:

1. How do you see God at work in the life of Joseph?

2. What would your response to God have been if your brothers plotted your murder and then you were falsely accused and banished to prison?

3. What do you think Joseph meant when he said, "What you meant for evil, God meant for good"?

4. What circumstance in your life right now is the most difficult to trust God with? Ask God for help in trusting Him.

CHAPTER 4

THE EYE OF THE STORM: MORE THAN CONQUERORS

BY STEVE D. WHITAKER, PhD

*"Now faith is confidence in what we hope for
and assurance about what we do not see."*

HEBREWS 11:1

DURING OUR GREATEST life struggles or "storms,"
we look to others who have successfully prevailed
through trials. They become our heroes who give us the
strength to persevere. The Bible is brimming with stories
of real-life God-followers who struggled or suffered and

then witnessed God come through in miraculous ways. Human history also records similar God-fearing individuals who inspire us to press on in faith.

WALK BY FAITH—NOAH

No one has ever seen rain.

He couldn't push that thought out of his head as he worked side-by-side with his three sons. No rain had ever touched the earth. He wondered what rain would be like. It was hard to imagine droplets of water falling out of the heavens, even for a wise man like Noah.

His neighbors didn't understand what he was doing. Sometimes Noah himself didn't understand. He spent his entire life loving his family and walking with God. As far as he could see, his steadfastness had led only to public mockery and serious doubt.

Noah knew no one outside his home who sought after the Lord. He had felt alone in his town for years. God said that He would fix the problem. He said that Noah's faith was going to save him. Noah believed God. He just didn't understand how building an ark was going to solve any problems.

And to think of how he would corral all those animals. Talk about a mess.

Maybe he was crazy. Maybe no rain would come, as everyone else predicted. But maybe something incredible was ahead for his family and for all mankind that Noah couldn't begin to imagine.

He had faith. He knew his work and his words seemed like nonsense to the scoffers around him. In the midst of his doubts, he had a steady peace in his heart. After all, God hadn't let him down yet.[45]

At the appointed time, Noah closed the door to the ark. He shared the ark with his wife, his sons, their wives, and two of every sort of animal that lived on the face of the earth.

God sent rain upon the earth for forty days and forty nights. Not only that, but the fountains of water under the surface of the earth broke open, and the world was engulfed in an epic flood. In this stunning reversal of creation, the entire earth was submerged in water. For 150 days, even the tops of the highest mountains remained covered with more than 22 feet of water.

After nearly 10 months at sea, the waters on the earth finally dried. Noah finally stepped on solid ground. The rain had come after all. The water flooded the earth and destroyed everything.

It was decades before Noah saw the fullness of God's promise come into effect. Even then, he knew his family had to start over. They were alone on the earth.

God kept His promise. Noah knew He wouldn't fail. The world had been saved through his obedience, even though he didn't understand. Nothing about the journey had been easy. Despite that, Noah knew it was worth every hard moment.

God kept His promise.

In the years that followed, he would look up to the sky and see a colorful promise from God. He would never have to build another ark or watch his neighbors die. God was going to restore what had been lost.

The remainder of Noah's life would not be without difficulties and mistakes. God hadn't chosen this man because he was perfect. God chose Noah because he was faithful in the midst of a broken culture. He walked with God.[60]

FOR SUCH A TIME AS THIS—ESTHER

One of my favorite characters in all of Scripture is a woman by the name of Esther. Esther was plucked from obscurity and placed into royalty as the wife of the Persian king, Xerxes. She was a Jew, while her husband was a Gentile. Shortly after her arrival in the court of the king, she was confronted with a crisis. Mordecai, her cousin and former protector, faced death at the hands of Haman, a chief officer of the Persian state.

Haman hatched a plot to exterminate all Jews from the kingdom. Upon hearing reports of this sinister plan, Esther sought counsel from Mordecai. He spoke words of wisdom to the newly appointed queen, advising her to inform the king: "If you keep silent at this time, relief and deliverance will rise for the Jews from another place, but you and your father's house will perish. And who knows whether you have not come to the kingdom for such a time as this?" (Esther 4:14)."[61]

Esther showed the tenderness of a lamb and the boldness of a lion. She approached the king without invitation, an offense punishable by death, and interceded on behalf of her people. The king was pleased to come to the aid of the Jews and did so by dismissing and executing the wicked Haman.

The story of Esther serves as a call to action. We have much in common with this queen. John Piper, chancellor of Bethlehem College & Seminary in Minneapolis, highlights these similarities by noting, "We live in a place of privilege. We have access to channels of power and influence. We have wealth and resources that can be used for causes greater than ourselves. The question for Esther was the same as it is for us: 'Why has God entrusted us with all of these things?' The answer: He has done so for such a time as this."[62]

LEAD WITH A HUMBLE HEART— GEORGE WASHINGTON

Before George Washington became the first president of the United States (from 1789 to 1797), he served as a general leading unlikely warriors into battle against a world superpower. Victory was unlikely.

Through these battles, the victory, and his subsequent presidency, Washington exemplified what it means to be a humble leader. He lived through extraordinary highs and discouraging lows. "The American Experiment" was risky and different from any political system before it.

American writer and historian Ron Chernow details how reluctant Washington was to become America's first president, but through hindsight we see how gracefully he served our developing nation. In his humility, Washington

Our sinful human nature is not inclined toward humility.

never wavered when he believed that he was doing something right, no matter how difficult it was.[47]

Our sinful human nature is not inclined toward humility. We live in a world of Kardashians, YouTube, and selfies. My generation has been called the "me generation," and my children's generation has been graced with the title of the "me me me generation." America is the land we call home, and nowadays this land is one of instant gratification for any of our many wants.[48]

In the midst of hard times, George Washington paved the way with humility and grace. Being faithful in the small areas does not mean we relinquish our values or our constitutional rights.

In his wisdom and humility, Washington once said, "If the freedom of speech is taken away, then dumb and silent we may be led, like sheep to the slaughter."[49]

Using Washington's life and character as an example, we can be encouraged. We do not have to know how the story of our country ends. We don't even need to know how tomorrow will end. We only need to do the next right thing. We have to make the next good choice. Through it all, we must be humble enough to point back to the one who makes our lives possible.

PRESS ON—WILLIAM WILBERFORCE

Not long after George Washington, a British man named William Wilberforce demonstrated patience and perseverance in a remarkable manner. He saw slavery abolished in England mere months before his death in 1833. He had been fighting toward this end for nearly five decades.[50]

His indefatigable spirit is one rarely demonstrated in our current culture. He fought his way through criticism and self-doubt as a Christian in Parliament.

One thing that set Wilberforce apart was his passionate pursuit of Christ in a culture that did not understand genuine Christianity. Wilberforce called out the apathy and the misunderstanding of sin so prevalent in the lives of those around him.[51] Without a doubt, he engaged and challenged his community. However, he also loved and served them throughout his political career.

"He was a radically God-centered Christian who was a politician," John Piper wrote about Wilberforce.[52]

I regret that I can't think of many in the political arena today who fit this description. However, I can see the same struggles Wilberforce faced as ones present in today's culture. To be a Christian today is framed as fanaticism or lunacy by the secular media, by politicians in each political party, and in popular forms of entertainment. Sometimes it feels easier to retreat and hide at home, school, or church. As Wilberforce did, perhaps we should take the words of John Newton to heart: "It is hoped and believed the Lord has raised you up for the good of His church and for the good of the nation."[53]

STAND FOR SOMETHING—ERIC LIDDELL

Scottish athlete and missionary Eric Liddell once said, "Circumstances may appear to wreck our lives and God's plans, but God is not helpless among the ruins. God's love is still working. He comes in and takes the calamity and uses it victoriously, working out His wonderful plan of love."[56]

The Academy Award-winning movie *Chariots of Fire* was based on the life of Liddell, an Olympic runner and missionary to China. His life provides powerful lessons for us to learn.

Liddell, who was born in 1902 and died in 1945, was uncompromising. In a world where everyone tries to find the easy way out or the fastest way to get ahead, it's hard to imagine crossing paths with someone as steadfast as Eric Liddell. He refused to run in the 1924 Olympic event he had been training for, the 100-meter, because it took place on Sunday—the Sabbath.[57] If I were an athlete, I don't know that I would have been as firm in my convictions.

In spite of his sacrifice, Liddell won a gold medal for the 400-meter race, which he chose to run instead. God honored his hard work and his commitment. Instead of pursuing an athletic career, Liddell chose to serve on the mission field like his parents did before him. He died from the effects of a brain tumor while serving in a foreign country proclaiming the Gospel.

No matter what we face personally or nationally, nothing comes as a surprise to God. He is still sovereign over all. He is good, loving, and faithful through the best and the worst of times.

HE IS ALL I NEED—CORRIE TEN BOOM

Corrie ten Boom is a perfect example of a woman who was both gentle toward others and firm in her faith, despite unimaginable suffering. The author of *The Hiding Place* hid Jewish men and women along with other members of the Nazi resistance for as long as she could at her home in the Netherlands. Eventually Corrie and her sister, Betsie, were arrested and sent to a Nazi concentration camp in 1944.

Amid all her hardship and the loss of several family members, Corrie kept her faith in God. In a way I struggle to fathom, she trusted in His goodness and His sovereign will until her miraculous release from prison.[58]

Even though it seems like the moral light of our country grows dimmer and dimmer, we must hold to the same kind of gentleness and intense faith Corrie ten Boom showed throughout her life, whether her circumstances were positive or negative. She wisely said, "You can never learn that Christ is all you need until Christ is all you have."[59]

THE PEACEFUL PURSUIT OF A DREAM—MARTIN LUTHER KING

In the 1950s and 1960s, an American hero was fighting for human rights. Although slavery had been abolished in America, African-American citizens were still being treated without the full rights and privileges of citizens or image-bearers of God. Dr. Martin Luther King Jr.'s renowned dream came to fruition through peaceful resistance. In his Letter from Birmingham Jail in 1963, he describes why peaceful resistance is the best response to oppression.[54]

Even though American Christians are not oppressed like those who suffered through segregation, followers of Jesus have been persecuted since the time He walked the earth. We will continue to face resistance and ridicule until He returns.

Of the earliest Christians, Dr. King said, "They were too God-intoxicated to be 'astronomically intimidated.'" The focus was not about the suffering they went through—it was all about the cause of Christ. They were seen as "extreme," King observed, but they were extreme for the right causes.

In Dr. King's letter, we can see that many of his observations of society are reflected in our society as well. Many of his followers probably

We should emulate this example of peaceful resistance.

felt the way we do—that our world is going downhill and there is no good way out. Dr. King saw the world differently. He believed he could make a difference. He believed in justice and quiet determination.

Martin Luther King, Jr., was put in jail for doing what he knew was right. He didn't lead violent protests or spew hateful rhetoric. He preached a message of love and hope without compromising his convictions.

In times of prosperity and in moments of persecution, we anchor deep and trust our Father in heaven. We believe in the sovereignty of God, and we know that it is His hand that directs our steps. Today you chose to pick up this book and read it, which means God is at work in your life. He wants to do something special in and through you.

CHAPTER SUMMARY

The account of Noah in the book of Genesis shows us that choosing to follow God may require us to perform actions that the world around us will not understand. God will reward our faithfulness. Just as the rainbow in the sky promised all mankind would never suffer another flood, our faithfulness might also have far-reaching effects that will last for generations.

Hebrews 11 describes biblical heroes who triumphed even in the midst of tragedy. In this chapter, we learn a great deal from these people of strong faith. From their lives, and from modern-day Esthers and Noahs, we find the confidence to accomplish the following:

- Risk all that we have for such a time as this—Queen Esther
- Lead with a humble heart—George Washington
- Press on, no matter how long and arduous the fight—William Wilberforce
- Stand firm on our conviction, no matter what others think—Eric Liddell

- Believe that Jesus is all we need—Corrie ten Boom
- Face the opposition in a peaceful manner—Martin Luther King, Jr.

Key verse: "But as it is, they desire a better country, that is, a heavenly one. Therefore God is not ashamed to be called their God, for he has prepared for them a city" (Hebr. 11:16).

FAMILY MINUTE

When we look to the past, we see a long line of faithful followers of God who stood strong in the midst of trying circumstances. Each one has strong character that we can emulate as we go through our own tumultuous journeys. They walked by faith, which Hebrews 11:1 says is having "confidence in what we hope for and assurance about what we do not see." Read the biographical stories in this chapter and ask the following questions:

1. In what ways do you identify with the difficulties faced by the main character in each story?

2. How did he or she demonstrate faith in God, even in the midst of tough times?

3. What kind of tough times or difficulties do you think Christians may face in the days ahead?

4. How do you think God wants us to respond to turbulent times?

CHAPTER 5

STRONGER BECAUSE OF THE WIND: GROW DEEP ROOTS

By Steve D. Whitaker, PhD

"Let your speech always be gracious, seasoned with salt, so that you may know how you ought to answer each person."

Colossians 4:6

Have you ever heard of the Biodome Project? The designers of the experiment attempted to create a perfectly controlled environment intended to produce ideal fruits and vegetation.

Among the many failures in the project, scientists discovered that once trees reached a certain height, they toppled over. The problem was that there was not enough wind in the Biodome.[63]

For trees to grow strong and develop robust root systems, there must be winds that bend and bow the branches. The stress of wind and rain causes the root system to grow deeper and stronger, which in turn allows the tree to grow taller.

Harsh winds produce strong root systems.

As we've seen in previous chapters, the Bible gives many examples of persons who flourished as a result of the strength and depth of their faith. Likewise, the story of America is a testimony to the fact that harsh winds produce strong root systems.

MORE THAN A SHEPHERD BOY—DAVID

The Bible tells the story of a man called David who understood this principle. Through the harshest storms and the darkest nights, he prevailed. He conquered overwhelming fear and overcame enormous odds. He experienced adversity at an early age and was called a "man after God's own heart."[64]

"David, wake up." The morning light, once hidden by the closed flap on the side of the tent, streamed through. David slowly awoke and saw the familiar silhouette of his father, Jesse.

"Wake up and wash your face. You need to gather your things and begin your journey," his dad said. "This sack is full of grain. The other sack contains bread and cheese. As we discussed last night, I want you to take these provisions to your brothers in the Valley of Elah. They are fighting against an evil army, and your mother and I are worried about their safety. We pray that you return with a good report."[65]

David was 14 years of age, and this was every boy's dream. He was going to watch a live battle. Swords and spears. Horses and chariots. He was going to see the bravery of his older brothers on display before his very eyes. Sure, it was going to take him two days to get there, but something deep inside told him this was going to be the adventure of a lifetime.

He knew the terrain well from tending his father's sheep. There were dangerous cliffs, and the land was populated with unfriendly wildlife. In spite of this, he found himself enjoying the time alone as he navigated his way along the dusty trail. No sheep to rescue. No lions to fight. No bears to kill. Just a shepherd boy and his thoughts.

As he lay his head down on the sack of grain that night to sleep, he looked up at the stars. They were more numerous than he could count. At this point he forgot about his arduous journey and instead marveled at the handiwork of the Creator. His eyelids were heavy as he repeated the Shema, "Hear, O Israel: The Lord our God, the Lord is one! You shall love the Lord your God with all your heart and with all your soul and with all your might."

It may have been on that very night that he first contemplated the words he later recorded as Psalm 8:[66]

> When I look at your heavens, the work of your fingers,
> the moon and the stars, which you have set in place,
> what is man that you are mindful of him, and the son
>   of man that you care for him?

Yet you have made him a little lower than the heavenly
    beings
and crowned him with glory and honor.
You have given him dominion over the works of your
    hands;
you have put all things under his feet,
all sheep and oxen, and also the beasts of the field,
the birds of the heavens, and the fish of the sea,
    whatever passes along the paths of the seas.
O Lord, our Lord, how majestic is your name in all
    the earth!

David woke early the next morning. He was still several hours away from Elah. As the sun rose over the mountains, he knelt down at the edge of a small stream feeding into the valley below. As he splashed water on his face, he noticed an unusually plentiful supply of smooth stones ideally suited for his sling.

In the quiet of the morning, he walked and talked with God. He recited the prayers he had learned at the feet of his mother. His mind quickly jumped to the recent visit his family had enjoyed from the prophet Samuel. He was still trying to make sense of everything the prophet had said to his father:

"And Jesse made seven of his sons pass before Samuel. And Samuel said to Jesse, 'The Lord has not chosen these.' Then Samuel said to Jesse, 'Are all your sons here?' And he said, 'There remains yet the youngest, but behold, he is keeping the sheep.' And Samuel said to Jesse, 'Send and get him, for we will not sit down till he comes here.' And he sent and brought him in. Now he was ruddy and had beautiful eyes and was handsome. And the Lord said, 'Arise, anoint him, for this is he.' Then Samuel took the horn of oil and anointed him in the midst of his brothers. And the Spirit of the Lord rushed upon David from that day forward. And Samuel rose up and went to Ramah."[67]

Suddenly David snapped back to reality. To the south, he saw the Philistines armed for battle. A few hundred yards ahead, he saw the Israelites poised for battle as well. Both armies seemed overwhelmed with commotion near the stream that ran between the mountain ridges. In the middle of the valley stood a man suited with armor and larger than any living creature David had ever seen.

He had learned of the legend of Goliath, and now he watched in horror as the giant mocked his fellow countrymen and blasphemed the name of the Lord. David was outraged by what he heard and saw. Fear gripped his heart. His knees buckled in weakness. He reached for his sling.[68]

As quickly as the anxiety had arrived, it disappeared. It was replaced by an unexplainable sense of peace, purpose, and determination.

It was the same feeling that came upon him when the prophet had anointed him with oil. He dropped his belongings and walked toward the front lines. His brothers pleaded with him to stop. The officers tried to arm him with a shield, sword, and spear. But David wanted none of it. The Spirit of the Lord was upon him.

With five smooth stones in one hand and a sling in the other, he walked toward Goliath. The giant laughed. David whispered a prayer. Goliath reached for his spear. David reached for a stone.

> "Then the Philistine said to David, 'Am I a dog, that you come to me with sticks?' The Philistine further said, 'Come to me, and I will give your flesh to the birds of the air and to the beasts of the field.' Then David said to the Philistine, 'You come to me with a sword and with a spear and with a javelin, but I come to you in the name of

the Lord of hosts, the God of the armies of Israel, whom you have defied. This day the Lord will deliver you into my hand, and I will strike you down and cut off your head. And I will give the dead bodies of the host of the Philistines this day to the birds of the air and to the wild beasts of the earth, that all the earth may know that there is a God in Israel, and that all this assembly may know that the Lord saves not with sword and spear. For the battle is the Lord's, and He will give you into our hand.'

"And David put his hand in his bag and took out a stone and slung it and struck the Philistine on his forehead. The stone sank into his forehead, and he fell on his face to the ground."[69]

You know the rest of the story. David killed Goliath. The Philistine army fled, and Israel won the battle. In the midst of a turbulent time, David anchored his hope to the King of kings and Lord of lords.

THE BIRTH OF A NATION

The American colonists of the 1700s felt like David. They viewed their British ruler as Goliath.

It was March 23, 1775, at the third Virginia convention, held at St. John's Church in Richmond. King George had recently declared all 13 North American colonies to be in a state of open rebellion. Lord Dunsmore, the Royal Governor of Virginia, had ordered all the gunpowder in Williamsburg seized and stored aboard his ship anchored in the Virginia harbor to keep it out of the hands of local patriot forces.

The hopes of the early settlers who dreamed of liberty and freedom seemed to be fading under the strong hand of Great Britain. In this setting, Patrick Henry spoke the words that still resonate in the hearts and minds of freedom-loving Americans: "There is a just God who presides over the destinies of nations...Is life so dear or peace so sweet as to be purchased at the price of chains and slavery? Forbid it, Almighty God! I know not what course others may take; but as for me, give me liberty or give me death."[70]

Because the founders of our nation persisted through perilous times, we live in the greatest country on the planet. We are able to worship openly. We can work hard and achieve success like nowhere else in the world. We boast of the most developed medical technology in the history of civilization. Our military is viewed as the most powerful of all nations. Our education system, though not perfect, is still the envy of the world. These blessings were forged in a crucible of oppression, hatred, and persecution.

Washington, Henry, and Franklin anchored deep in turbulent times. They created a system of government rooted in a belief that God exists and rules over the affairs of men.

Ben Franklin said, "I've lived, sir, a long time, and the longer I live, the more convincing proofs I see of this truth: that God governs in the affairs of men. If a sparrow cannot fall to the ground without His notice, it is improbable that an empire can rise without His aid. We've been assured in the sacred writings that unless the Lord builds the house, they labor in vain who build it. I firmly believe this, and I also believe that without His concurring aid, we shall succeed in this political building no better than the builders of Babel."[71]

The first president of the United States, George Washington, believed, "It is the duty of all nations to acknowledge the providence of Almighty God, to obey

His will, to be grateful for His benefits, and humbly implore His protection and favor."[72]

STEWARDING A LEGACY

We pledge allegiance to the American flag to instill a deep appreciation for our nation and bolster the idea of patriotism. We celebrate Veteran's Day to pay tribute to fallen servicemen and women. On September 11, we recognize those who lost their lives in the most brutal attack on American soil.

Nowadays, the forces of secularism are waging war against traditional Christian values. In some respects, Christ-followers feel like David the Shepherd Boy or the Sons of Liberty. We are torn between taking a stand and being paralyzed by fear.

We must hold fast to our patriotic traditions.

Catholic talk-show host and author Hugh Hewitt writes, "Even as political forces gather to effectively expel people of faith from the public life, the abilities of those who would gladly fight for their right to remain in the public square are strongly diminished. Though a treasure of examples is laid up—the gentleness of St. Francis of Assisi, the determination of Dietrich Bonhoeffer, the learning of Thomas Moore, and the persistence of William Wilberforce—the church is running out of talent or steam or both."[73]

We must hold fast to our patriotic traditions and be good stewards of the legacy we've been given. We must do our part to leave the Republic better than we found it for the sake of the next generation.

How do we do that? In the midst of the turbulent times we live in, and in light of what we believe about the Gospel, where do we go from here?

The answer is not to run and hide. The solution is not to be shrill and offensive.

We need a few Davids who have encountered the living God in a personal way—young men and women who aren't looking for power, position, or privilege but are willing to serve, no matter the cost. We need patriots who possess a paradoxical blend of personal humility and well-founded confidence that Truth can and will prevail. We need a thoughtful and deliberate approach that rests on this firm foundation: *in God we trust*.

CREATE YOUR ACTION PLAN

As we began this journey together, we set three simple goals. First, it was our intention to challenge Christ-followers to gain a fresh awareness of the decay within our culture. Second, our desire was to point you toward the source of our hope and His sovereign rule in our lives. Finally, we wanted to inspire believers to fashion a grace-filled response to the overwhelming needs in our country.

In the closing pages of this book, we want to offer you a plan for cultural engagement. We do so boldly, believing that "the Lord has established his throne in the heavens, and his kingdom rules over all."[74] We do so confidently, understanding that "the light shines in the darkness, and the darkness has not overcome it."[75]

> *Let the winds and waves produce deep roots in your life.*

Let the winds and waves produce deep roots in your life. When we are secured by Truth, Christ-like character, wisdom, unwavering faith, and prayer, we can withstand the strongest storms the enemy can muster.

The plan for cultural engagement calls us to embrace five simple principles:

1. *We need to focus on Truth rather than trivialities.* We must consider how the positions of our political leaders align with biblical Truth rather than focusing on our personal preferences or political affiliations. There will be no perfect leaders because there are no perfect men and women. This reality seems to be on constant display in the political arena as we witness duplicity, arrogance, and manipulation. Our task is not to align with a political ideology or person but to prayerfully discern which political leaders will most fervently support the Constitution and religious liberty.

2. *We need to demonstrate the character of Christ in our words, actions, and deeds.* The secular media are quick to highlight Christians who fail to walk the walk. For that reason, we must not engage in character assassination of those we disagree with nor use bombastic words or antics laced with hateful undertones. Those who see the world through a lens other than Christianity are still precious in the sight of their Creator. He loves them. We must extend grace and kindness

to them, regardless of their political affiliations, religious preferences, or personal behaviors.

3. *We need to boldly engage the political process in a responsible and informed manner.* We believe this is part of being the "aroma of Christ."[76] Study the issues carefully, and take time to refine your thoughts in writing. Contrast your beliefs with the opposing point of view, and test your thinking using the arguments of your opponents. Once you are confident in your position, find a place for your voice to be heard, and season your words with compassion and concern rather than criticism. Simply stated, let's learn to present a compelling argument and practice the art of disagreeing agreeably.

4. *We need to remember that God appoints the rulers of all societies.* While we care deeply about our faith and our country, we will not presume to declare who God's favorite political party or leader might be. The Bible reminds us, "It is God who judges: He brings one down, he exalts another"[77] and "He

changes times and seasons; he deposes kings and raises up others. He gives wisdom to the wise and knowledge to the discerning."[78]

5. *We need to pray faithfully for our elected officials and those pursuing office.* Charles Spurgeon, the "Prince of Preachers," said, "Prayer is the slender nerve that moves the omnipotent muscle of God."[79] The Bible tells us in Proverbs 21:1, "The king's heart is a stream of water in the hand of the Lord; he turns it wherever he will." The apostle Paul admonishes believers, saying, "I exhort therefore, that, first of all, supplications, prayers, intercessions, and giving of thanks be made for all men; for kings, and for all that are in authority; that we may lead a quiet and peaceable life in all godliness and honesty."[80]

READY FOR THE STORM

There's no disputing that we live in turbulent times. We are already feeling the outer bands of a massive storm that seeks to upend the institutions and ideals that

Christ-followers have treasured for generations. Some are well aware and are making preparations. Others haven't a clue.

It's time to dust off that hurricane map, put a game plan together, and anchor deep. Your children are watching. Your friends and neighbors are studying your countenance. They're looking for answers. Don't miss this opportunity to be the hands and feet of Jesus to a lost and dying world.

CHAPTER SUMMARY

We began this book by describing a serious problem (cultural decay). In the middle of the book, we looked at a remedy. In this chapter, we provide a plan of action. It's time for Christ-followers to be the hands and feet of Jesus. Today we are called to take heart, chart a course, and speak the Truth in love amid the chaos. These are the final lessons:

- The Body of Christ, the church, grows stronger in the face of opposition.

- The Bible is replete with stories of men and women who allowed persecution to make them better rather than bitter.

- Some of the greatest blessings we enjoy were birthed in the crucible of pain and pressure.

- Our response to turbulent times must be seasoned with grace and love.

Key verse: "I exhort therefore, that, first of all, supplications, prayers, intercessions, and giving of thanks be made for all men; For kings, and for all that are in authority; that we may lead a quiet and peaceable life in all godliness and honesty" (1 Tim. 2:1–2).

FAMILY MINUTE

Turbulent times often strengthen our character and lead to unexpected opportunities. Re-read the action plan at the end of this chapter, and ask these questions:

1. How can your family's collective response in these turbulent times give you a platform to share the Gospel with your unbelieving friends and neighbors?

2. What is an example of a turbulent time you or someone you know has endured? Read Psalm 46 together and discuss David's confidence in God during his turbulent times.

3. Referencing Psalm 8, list what you learn about God and about man. How does this list affect how you view your life and the lives of others?

FIVE ANCHOR POINTS IN TURBULENT TIMES

LET'S REVIEW THE five anchor points in turbulent times we just discussed in chapters 1 through 5. When you need a quick reminder of these effective strategies for weathering the storms of life, review these summary statements and key Bible verses.

1. HURRICANE WARNINGS: KNOW THE PATH OF THE STORM

Summary: As we face a quickly moving cultural storm of moral relativism, political conflicts, and religious persecution, we must analyze the strength of the winds and consider our own preparedness.

Key verse: "He said, 'Do not be afraid, for those who are with us are more than those who are with them'" (2 Kings 6:16).

2. ESSENTIAL PREPARATION: ANCHOR DEEP, AHEAD OF THE STORM

Summary: The world has many ideas about what can give us hope and what should be the source to which we anchor our lives. Only in Christ can we find true hope and the strongest foundation.

Key verse: "Some trust in chariots and some in horses, but we trust in the name of the Lord our God" (Ps. 20:7).

3. WHEN THE WAVES START CRASHING: PUT TRUST TO THE TEST

Summary: Even if our circumstances seem bleak and we don't see how we can survive, God has a way of turning difficulties into something good that glorifies His name.

Key verse: "As for you, you meant evil against me, but God meant it for good, to bring it about that many people should be kept alive, as they are today" (Gen. 50:20).

4. THE EYE OF THE STORM: MORE THAN CONQUERORS

Summary: When we look to the past, we see a long line of faithful Christ-followers who stood strong in the midst of persecution. Each one has strong character that we can emulate as we go through our own tumultuous journeys.

Key verse: "Now faith is the assurance of things hoped for, the conviction of things not seen" (Hebr. 11:1).

5. STRONGER BECAUSE OF THE WIND: GROW DEEP ROOTS

Summary: Turbulent times will strengthen our character and our relationships if we are anchored properly.

Key verse: "First of all, then, I urge that supplications, prayers, intercessions, and thanksgivings be made for all people, for kings, and all who are in high positions, that we may lead a peaceful and quiet life, godly and dignified in every way" (1 Tim. 2:1–2).

SEVEN-DAY PRAYER JOURNEY

THIS SEVEN-DAY PRAYER guide is designed to be a model for prayer that can be repeated on a weekly basis. The structure is designed around relationships. We begin the week by praying for the people in most dire need of God's help—ourselves. As the week progresses, our focus extends outward to our spouses, our kids, our communities, and eventually to the world.

God did not leave us powerless. In fact, one of our greatest resources for hope, encouragement, protection, and strength is prayer. Jesus made a regular practice of finding time to be alone, praying to His Father, and asking for help for Himself and those He loved.

Our prayer for you is that as you work through this guide, you will be encouraged to go even deeper in your prayer life. This guided-prayer section is designed to be the beginning, so let it prompt you to share your heart with our loving God and go even deeper.

DAY 1: YOURSELF

Psalm 119:17–18: "Deal bountifully with your servant, that I may live and keep your word. Open my eyes, that I may behold wondrous things out of your law."

Guided prayer: Lord Jesus, I know that I must first see You before I am able to see others accurately. If I miss You, God, I miss everything. If I don't hear what You want me to hear, I am lost. So please, God, open the eyes of my heart that I may see You as You truly are: wonderful, majestic, powerful, kind, forgiving, patient, and glorious. Help me be attuned to the words that are coming from You. Help me speak words that are peacemaking, words that help others see Your grace and love for them.

DAY 2: YOUR SPOUSE

Philippians 2:3: "Do nothing from selfish ambition or empty pride, but in humility consider others more important than yourselves."

Guided prayer: Father God, You came to earth as a servant, and You call those who follow You to serve others. At times the hardest person to truly serve is my spouse. I ask that by Your strength, you will help me view his/her needs above my own, to place his/her wants and desires above my own, and to love him/her through humble service. Help our marriage be a marriage that honors You and demonstrates Your love to a hurting world. On the really difficult days, help us be patient and kind with each other as You are patient and kind with us.

DAY 3: YOUR KIDS/GRANDKIDS

3 John 1:3–4: "For I rejoiced greatly when the brothers came and testified to your truth, as indeed you are walking in the truth. I have no greater joy than to hear that my children are walking in the truth."

Guided prayer: Heavenly Father, in a world that is constantly doubting truth and offering up false truths, I pray that You would help my children/grandchildren have wisdom from You that allows them to see You, the only Truth. Help them not only understand the Truth with their minds, but to love it with their hearts. Keep them from deception. Father, I have no greater joy than when my kids walk in Your Truth, so please help them do that very thing.

DAY 4: YOUR CHURCH

Philippians 1:3–6: "I thank my God in all my remembrance of you, always, in every prayer of mine for you all making my prayer with joy because of your partnership in the gospel from the first day until now. And I am sure of this, that he who began a good work in you will bring it to completion at the day of Jesus Christ."

Guided prayer: Lord Jesus, in Your Word, You promise that nothing will overcome Your church. Yet in these turbulent times, it seems as though Your church is being attacked from every angle. Help us, Your beloved, to know your strength. Help us, Your bride, remain steadfast under pressure and be faithful to share the truth of Your Gospel with a hurting world. Help us, Your church, love and know Your Truth and stay committed to following it.

DAY 5: YOUR COMMUNITY

Jeremiah 29:7: "But seek the welfare of the city where I have sent you into exile, and pray to the Lord on its behalf, for in its welfare you will find your welfare."

Guided prayer: Father God, You have always called Your people to love their neighbors. All of their neighbors. Father, I pray for those in my city who do not know You. Those who do not have enough to eat. Those who do not have a place to call home. As the God Who meets needs, I pray that You would meet these. I pray that You will provide me opportunities to be a part of these solutions. Father, as You challenged Your people living in Babylon to seek the good of the city, may I, my family, and my church be dedicated to seeing the good of the community we live in. Help us to be practical and compassionate in our service.

DAY 6: YOUR COUNTRY

1 Timothy 2:1–3: "First of all, then, I urge that supplications, prayers, intercessions, and thanksgivings be made for all people, for kings and all who are in high positions, that we may lead a peaceful and quiet life, godly and dignified in every way. This is good, and it is pleasing in the sight of God our Savior."

Guided prayer: Lord Jesus, You remind us that it is good and right to pray for those who are in authority over us. Yet we often find this difficult when we disagree with them for political reasons. Please help us separate the importance of praying for our leaders from our need to agree with them. Please give our leaders heavenly wisdom. Help them lead well and in such a way that will lead to the prosperity and freedom of our country. We are so thankful, Jesus, for the freedoms we have here in the United States. Continue to sustain these freedoms, and help us use our freedom to share the Good News with others boldly. Help us worship You boldly.

DAY 7: THE WORLD (OTHER NATIONS)

John 10:16: "And I have other sheep that are not of this fold. I must bring them also, and they will listen to my voice. So there will be one flock, one shepherd."

Guided prayer: Heavenly Father, we know that You sent Jesus on a rescue mission to save people from every part of the world. We know that it is Your desire that men, women, and children from all over the world would know and worship you. Help pastors and missionaries bring Your Good News to those who have not yet had an opportunity to hear it. Protect and help those Christians who live in countries that do not have the freedoms we enjoy in America. Encourage Your churches in countries where Christians are hated and despised. And continue to help those who hate Christianity see the beauty and truth in following You.

HELPFUL SCRIPTURE PROMISES FOR TURBULENT TIMES

THE BIBLE PROMISES that faith comes by hearing and hearing by the Word of God (Rom. 10:17). Our hope is that you will learn to trust these promises God has given and that they will become a source of hope and encouragement to you.

OUR ULTIMATE HOPE

Philippians 3:20: "But our citizenship is in heaven, and from it we await a Savior, the Lord Jesus Christ."

GOD'S LOVE NEVER CHANGES

Lamentations 3:22–23: "The steadfast love of the Lord never ceases; his mercies never come to an end."

GOD IS SOVEREIGN (IN CONTROL)

Romans 8:28: "And we know that for those who love God all things work together for good, for those who are called according to his purpose."

PRAY FOR OUR LEADERS

1 Timothy 2:1–2: "First of all, then, I urge that supplications, prayers, intercessions, and thanksgivings be made for all people, for kings and all who are in high positions, that we may lead a peaceful and quiet life, godly and dignified in every way."

TRUST, NOT WORRY

Matthew 6:34: "Therefore do not be anxious about tomorrow, for tomorrow will be anxious for itself. Sufficient for the day is its own trouble."

GOD CARES FOR YOU

1 Peter 5:6–7: "Humble yourselves, therefore, under the mighty hand of God so that at the proper time he may exalt you, casting all your anxieties on him, because he cares for you."

LIVE PEACEABLY WITH OTHERS

Romans 12:17–19: "Repay no one evil for evil, but give thought to do what is honorable in the sight of all. If possible, so far as it depends on you, live peaceably with all."

LOVE AND SERVE YOUR ENEMIES

Matthew 5:44: "But I say to you, love your enemies and pray for those who persecute you…"

Proverbs 25:21–22: "If your enemy is hungry, give him bread to eat, and if he is thirsty, give him water to drink, for you will heap burning coals on his head, and the Lord will reward you."

HONOR YOUR GOVERNMENT LEADERS

Romans 13:1–2: "Let every person be subject to the governing authorities. For there is no authority except from God, and those that exist have been instituted by God. Therefore whoever resists the authorities resists what God has appointed, and those who resist will incur judgment."

ENDNOTES

FOREWORD

1. George Barna, *Revolutionary Parenting: What the Research Shows Really Works* (Carol Stream, Illinois: Tyndale House Publishers, Inc., 2010).

2. Deuteronomy 6:4–5 (ESV).

INTRODUCTION

3. David Hoffman, "President Calls on Schools to Teach Basic Values," *The Washington Post* (August 24, 1984), 7.

4. "Obama and Clinton Love to Celebrate Gay Marriage Now: Here's How Late They Were to the Party," June 26, 2015, *The Washington Post*, https://www. washingtonpost.com/news/the-fix/wp/2015/06/26/ obama-and-clinton-love-to-celebrate-gay-marriage-now-heres-how-late-they-were-to-the-party/.

5. Todd Starnes, "Costly Beliefs: State Squeezes Last Penny from Bakers Who Defied Lesbian Wedding Cake Order," Fox News (December 29, 2015).

6. Todd Starnes, "Flower Power: Christian Florist Rejects Attorney General's Offer, Won't Betray Her Religious Beliefs," Fox News (February 23, 2015).

7. John Blake, "Ask the Card-Carrying Socialists: Is Obama One of Them?" CNN (April 15, 2010).

8. "Why So Many Millennials Are Socialists," Emily Ekins and Joy Pullmann, February 25, 2016, *The Federalist*, http://thefederalist.com/2016/02/15/why-so-many-millennials-are-socialists/.

9. Joseph Bottum, "The Death of Protestant America: A Political Theory of the Protestant Mainline," *First Things* (August 2008).

10. Todd Starnes, "School Sends Sheriff to Order Child to Stop Sharing Bible Verses," Fox News (June 3, 2016).

11. Joel Gehrke, "ACLU Lawyers Blame 'Christian Right,' GOP for Orlando Terrorist Attack," *Washington Examiner* (June 12, 2016).

12. "The Common-Sense Census: Media Use by Teens and Tweens," *The Common Sense* (2015).

13. James C. Dobson and Gary L. Bauer, *Children at Risk: The Battle for the Hearts and Minds of Our Kids* (Nashville: Word Publishing Group, 1990), 27.

14. Neil Postman, *Amusing Ourselves to Death: Public Discourse in the Age of Show Business* (New York: The Penguin Group, 2005).

15. "Against the Stream," Timothy George, October 1, 2012, *Christianity Today*, http://www.christianitytoday.com/ct/2012/september/againstthestream.html.

CHAPTER 1

16. Dobson and Bauer, *Children at Risk*, 103.

17. Maureen Dowd, "Playing the Jesus Card," *The New York Times* (December 15, 1999).

18. "What Would Jesus Do?" Roderick C. Meredith, March–April 2002, *Tomorrow's World*, http://www.tomorrowsworld.org/magazines/2002/march-april/what-would-jesus-do.

19. "Bush: Faith More Than a Sunday Formality," July 25, 2000, *USA Today*, http://usatoday30.usatoday.com/news/e98/e2248.htm.

20. Benjamin Wormald, "'Nones' on the Rise: New Report Finds One in Five Adults Have No Religious Affiliation," *Pew Research Centers Religion Public Life Project RSS* (October 9, 2012).

21. Samuel Smith, "Megachurches Seeing Drop in Weekly Attendance, Study Finds," *Christian Post* Online (December 3, 2015).

22. "State of the Bible 2016," American Bible Society, 2016.

23. Nancy Pearcey, *Total Truth: Liberating Christianity from Its Cultural Captivity* (Wheaton, Illinois: Crossway, 2004).

24. George Thomas Kurian and Mark A. Lamport (editors), *Encyclopedia of Christian Education, Volume 3* (London: Rowman and Littlefield, 2015), 295.

25. Isaiah 40:8 (ESV).

26. Michael S. Horton, *Made in America: The Shaping of Modern American Evangelicalism* (Eugene, Oregon: Wipf and Stock Publishers, 1991), 25.

27. Todd Starnes, "Florida School District Replaces Football Chaplains with Life Coaches," Fox News (August 27, 2014).

28. "Prayer in Schools," Carol Brooks, In Plain Site, http://www.inplainsite.org/what_happened_when_the_praying.html.

29. "Darrell Scott Testimony," David Mikkelson, Snopes, http://www.snopes.com/politics/guns/scott.asp.

30. David G. McCullough, *1776* (New York: Simon &Schuster, 2005).

31. 2 Kings 6:15–17 (MSG).

32. John 3:16 (ESV).

CHAPTER 2

33. Fyodor Dostoyevsky, Goodreads, http://www.goodreads.com/quotes/333739-prayer-is-the-slender-nerve-that-moves-the-muscle-of.

34. Melanie Haiken, "More Than 10,000 Suicides Tied to Economic Crisis, Study Says," *Forbes* (June 12, 2014).

35. Audi Q3 TV Spot, "Scripted Life," iSpot.tv, https://www.ispot.tv/ad/7r9e/2015-audi-q3-scripted-life.

36. Jeremiah 2:13 (ESV).

37. Edward Mote, "My Hope Is Built on Nothing Less," hymn, 1834, Hymnary.org, http://www.hymnary.org/text/my_hope_is_built_on_nothing_less.

38. 1 Peter 1:4 (ESV).

39. Psalm 20:7 (ESV).

40. Luke 2:36–38 (ESV).

CHAPTER 3

41. Genesis 37:3 (ESV).

42. Genesis 50:20 (ESV).

43. "Cultural Revolution," History.com, http://www.history.com/topics/cultural-revolution.

44. "China on Course to Become 'World's Most Christian Nation' Within Fifteen Years," Tom Phillips, *The Telegraph*, April 19, 2014, http://www.telegraph.co.uk/news/worldnews/asia/china/10776023/China-on-course-to-become-worlds-most-Christian-nation-within-15-years.html.

CHAPTER 4

45. Genesis 6–7 (ESV).

46. Genesis 15:6 (ESV).

47. "George Washington: The Reluctant President," Ron Chernow, *Smithsonian,* February 2011, http://www.smithsonianmag.com/ist/?next=/history/george-washington-the-reluctant-president-49492/.

48. "Millennials: The Me Me Me Generation," Joel Stein, *TIME*, May 20, 2013, http://time.com/247/millennials-the-me-me-me-generation/.

49. "National Gazette," George Washington's Mount Vernon website, http://www.mountvernon.org/digital-encyclopedia/article/national-gazette/.

50. "William Wilberforce," *Christianity Today*, http://www.christianitytoday.com/history/people/activists/william-wilberforce.html.

51. John Piper and Jonathan Aitken, *Amazing Grace in the Life of William Wilberforce* (Wheaton, Illinois: Crossway, 2007), 22–3.

52. Ibid., 25.

53. "Tribute to William Wilberforce, #1," John Piper, February 23, 2007, desiringGod, http://www.desiringgod.org/articles/tribute-to-william-wilberforce-1.

54. Stanford University, The Martin Luther King, Jr., Research and Education Institute, "Letter from a Birmingham Jail," April 16, 1963, http://kingencyclopedia.stanford.edu/encyclopedia/encyclopedia/enc_letter_from_birmingham_jail_1963/.

55. Acts 16:16–40 (ESV).

56. "Victory Over Circumstances," Eric Liddell, C. S. Lewis Institute, May 23, 2012, http://www.cslewisinstitute.org/Victory_Over_Circumstance_FullArticle.

57. "Harold Abrahams and Eric Liddell: Chariots of Fire," Encyclopedia Britannica Online, https://www.britannica.com/topic/1924-Olympic-Games-1117726.

58. Corrie ten Boom and John Sherrill, *The Hiding Place* (Ada, Michigan: Chosen Books, 1971).

59. Corrie ten Boom, Goodreads, http://www.goodreads.com/quotes/248538-you-can-never-learn-that-christ-is-all-you-need.

60. Genesis 9 (ESV).

61. Esther 4:14 (ESV).

62. Acts 13:22.

CHAPTER 5

63. "The Role of Wind in a Tree's Life," Anupum Pant, *Awesci Science Everyday,* December 28, 2014, http://awesci.com/the-role-of-wind-in-a-trees-life/.

64. Acts 13:22 (ESV).

65. 1 Samuel 17:17–18 (ESV).

66. Psalm 8:3–9 (ESV).

67. 1 Samuel 16:10–13 (ESV).

68. 1 Samuel 17:26–42 (ESV).

69. 1 Samuel 17:42–49 (ESV).

70. "Patrick Henry's 'Give Me Liberty or Give Me Death' Speech," History.org, https://www.history.org/almanack/life/politics/giveme.cfm.

71. "Founding Father's Quotes," *Founding Father's Quotes.*

72. "Washington's Thanksgiving Proclamation," David Mikkelson, Snopes, http://www.snopes.com/holidays/thanksgiving/washington.asp.

73. "Getting Ahead," Cindy Crosby, *Christianity Today*, August 1, 2003, http://www.christianitytoday.com/ct/2003/august/35.59.html.

74. Psalm 103:19 (ESV).

75. John 1:5 (ESV).

76. 2 Corinthians 2:15 (ESV).

77. Psalm 75:7 (ESV).

78. Daniel 2:21 (ESV).

79. Charles Spurgeon, Goodreads, http://www.goodreads.com/quotes/333739-prayer-is-the-slender-nerve-that-moves-the-muscle-of.

80. 1 Timothy 2:1 (ESV).